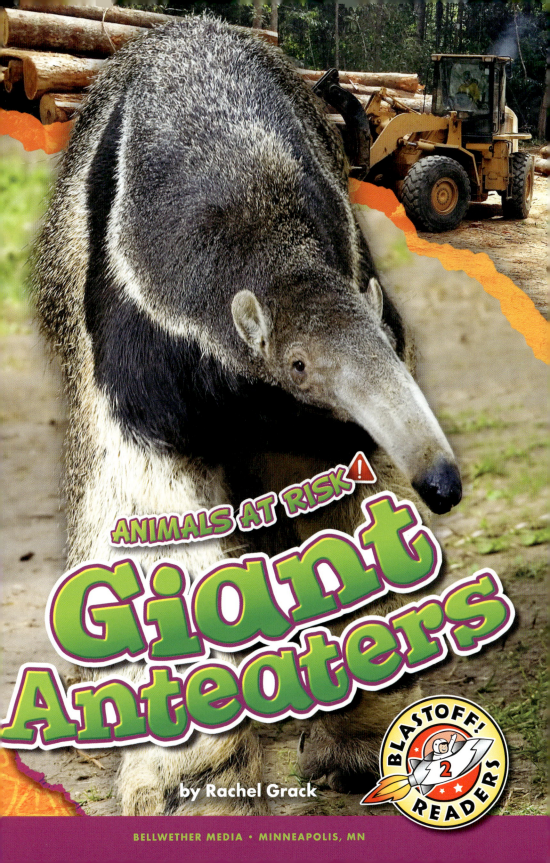

ANIMALS AT RISK

Giant Anteaters

by Rachel Grack

BLASTOFF! READERS 2

BELLWETHER MEDIA • MINNEAPOLIS, MN

Blastoff! Readers are carefully developed by literacy experts to build reading stamina and move students toward fluency by combining standards-based content with developmentally appropriate text.

 Level 1 provides the most support through repetition of high-frequency words, light text, predictable sentence patterns, and strong visual support.

 Level 2 offers early readers a bit more challenge through varied sentences, increased text load, and text-supportive special features.

 Level 3 advances early-fluent readers toward fluency through increased text load, less reliance on photos, advancing concepts, longer sentences, and more complex special features.

★ **Blastoff! Universe**

Reading Level

 Grade K  Grades 1–3   Grade 4

This edition first published in 2024 by Bellwether Media, Inc.

No part of this publication may be reproduced in whole or in part without written permission of the publisher. For information regarding permission, write to Bellwether Media, Inc., Attention: Permissions Department, 6012 Blue Circle Drive, Minnetonka, MN 55343.

Library of Congress Cataloging-in-Publication Data

Names: Koestler-Grack, Rachel A., 1973- author.
Title: Giant anteaters / Rachel Grack.
Description: Minneapolis, MN : Bellwether Media, 2024. | Series: Blastoff! Readers. Animals at risk | Includes bibliographical references and index. | Audience: Ages 5-8 | Audience: Grades 2-3 | Summary: "Relevant images match informative text in this introduction to giant anteaters. Intended for students in kindergarten through third grade"-- Provided by publisher.
Identifiers: LCCN 2023004258 (print) | LCCN 2023004259 (ebook) | ISBN 9798886874198 (library binding) | ISBN 9798886876079 (ebook)
Subjects: LCSH: Myrmecophaga--Juvenile literature. | Myrmecophaga--Conservation--Juvenile literature.
Classification: LCC QL737.E24 K64 2024 (print) | LCC QL737.E24 (ebook) | DDC 599.3/14--dc23/eng/20230130
LC record available at https://lccn.loc.gov/2023004258
LC ebook record available at https://lccn.loc.gov/2023004259

Text copyright © 2024 by Bellwether Media, Inc. BLASTOFF! READERS and associated logos are trademarks and/or registered trademarks of Bellwether Media, Inc.

Editor: Kieran Downs   Designer: Brittany McIntosh

Printed in the United States of America, North Mankato, MN.

Table of Contents

Nosy Eaters   4
In Danger!   8
Save the Giant Anteaters!   12
Glossary   22
To Learn More   23
Index   24

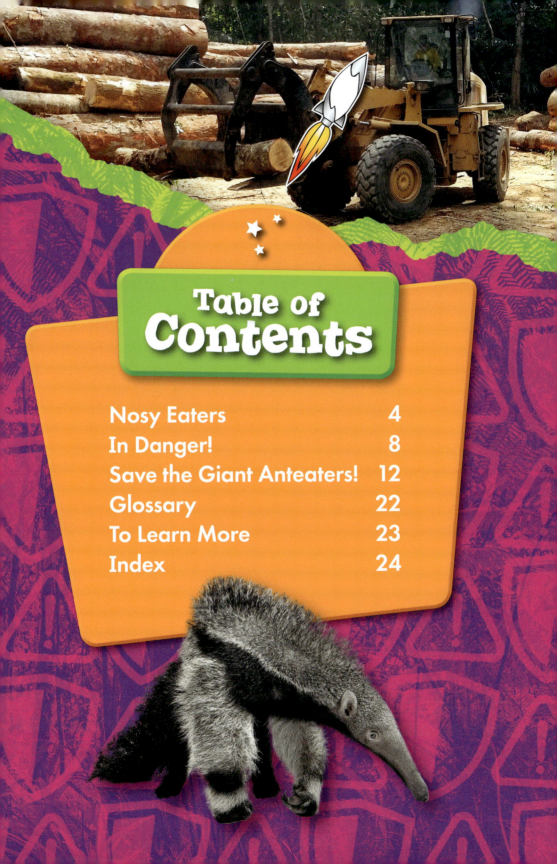

Nosy Eaters

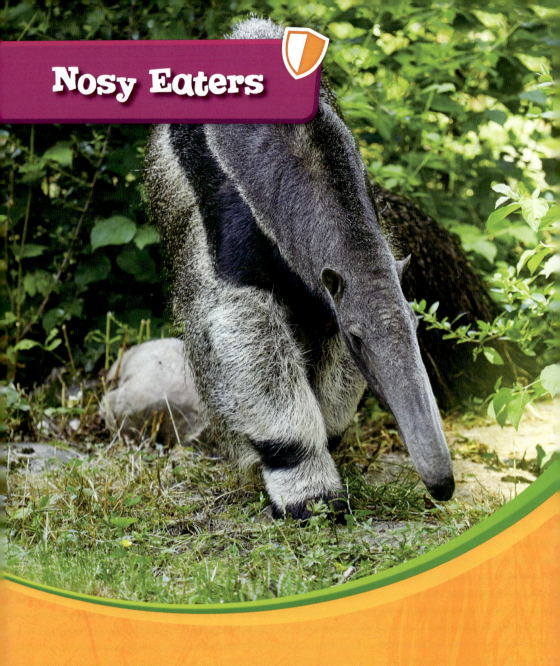

Giant anteaters are hairy animals with long, toothless **snouts**.

They are the largest of the four anteater **species**. They live in South and Central America.

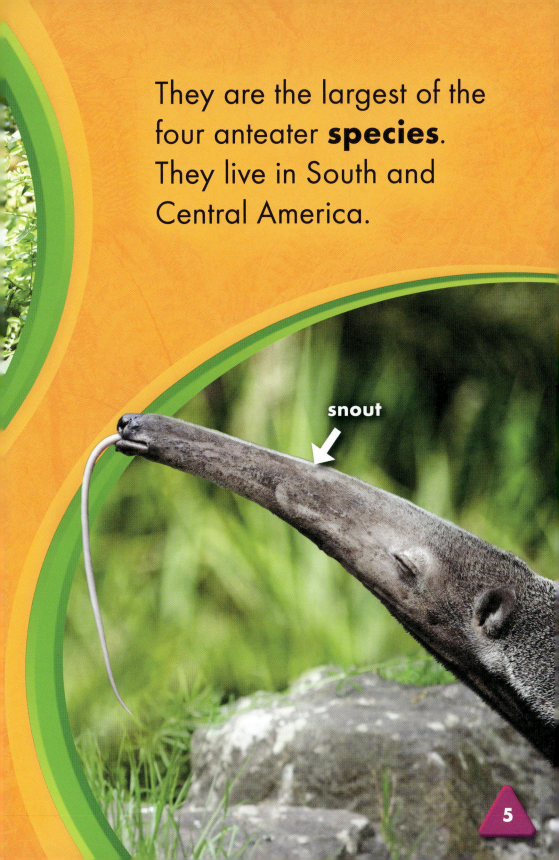

snout

Giant anteaters are found in several **habitats**. They **forage** in grasslands and forests.

But people are destroying their homes.

Giant Anteater Range

range =

In Danger!

Roads run through anteater homes. Giant anteaters often get hit by cars.

Farmers clear land where giant anteaters live. People hunt anteaters, too.

Threats

1. people need farmland

2. people clear forests

3. giant anteaters lose their homes

Some farmers burn their fields before planting. Fires spread into anteater habitats.

Dry weather from **climate change** also causes fires. Many giant anteaters have died.

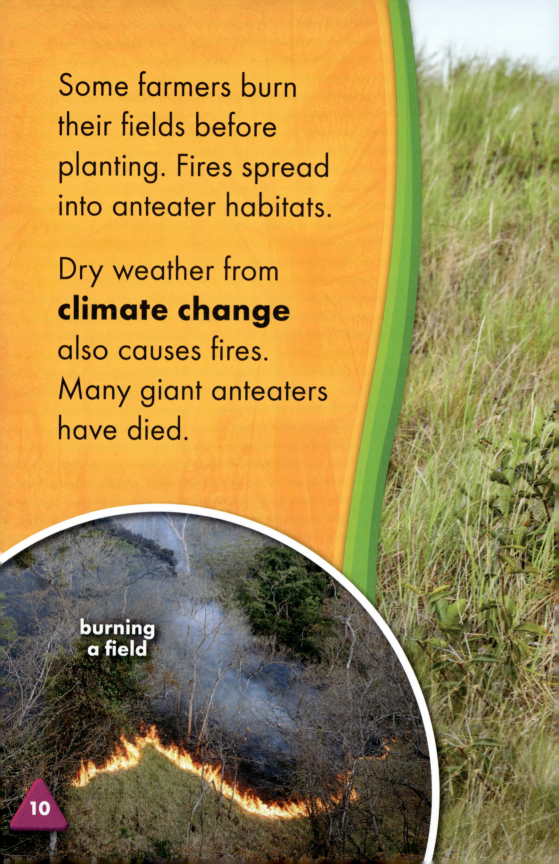

burning a field

Giant Anteater Stats

| Least Concern | Near Threatened | **Vulnerable** | Endangered | Critically Endangered | Extinct in the Wild | Extinct |

conservation status: vulnerable

life span: up to 14 years

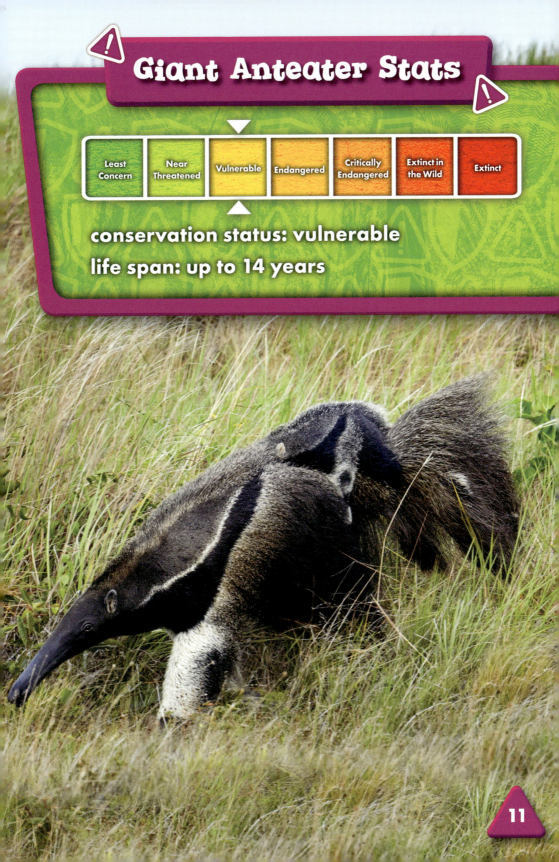

Save the Giant Anteaters!

termite mound

Giant anteaters are important to their **ecosystems**. They help control the number of ants and termites.

They are also food for larger animals.

The World with Giant Anteaters

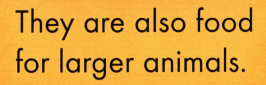

1 more giant anteaters

2 fewer ants and termites

3 healthy grasslands and forests

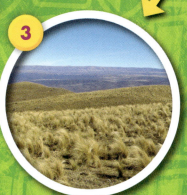

Governments pass **laws** to stop **deforestation**. They **protect** grasslands, too.

This keeps giant anteater homes safe.

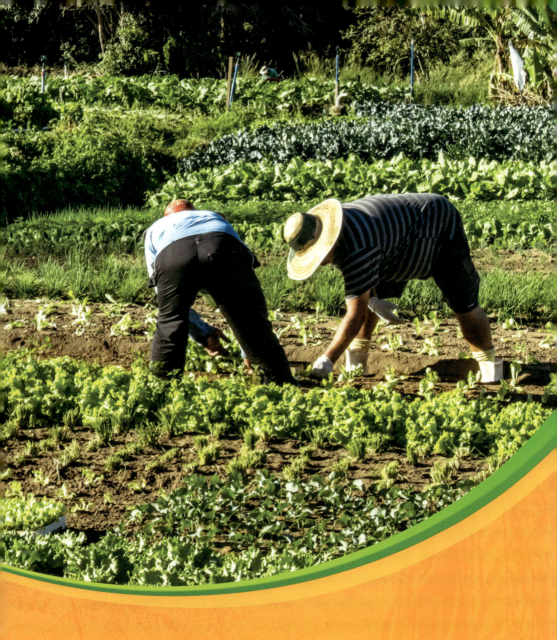

Farmers can prepare their fields without burning them. This stops fires from spreading.

They can learn new ways to grow crops on less land. Anteaters gain wider **home ranges**.

People study the movements of giant anteaters. They make pathways away from roads.

Giant anteaters stay safer from cars.

Walking or riding bikes instead of driving slows climate change. **Donations** to wildlife groups also help anteaters.

Everyone can help save giant anteaters!

Glossary

climate change—a human-caused change in Earth's weather due to warming temperatures

deforestation—the act of cutting down a wide area of trees

donations—gifts for a certain cause; most donations are money.

ecosystems—communities of plants and animals living in certain places

forage—to search for food

habitats—places and natural surroundings in which plants or animals live

home ranges—the lands on which groups of animals live and travel

laws—rules that must be followed

protect—to keep safe

snouts—the nose and mouth areas on animals

species—kinds of animals

To Learn More

AT THE LIBRARY

Gillespie, Katie. *Giant Anteater.* New York, N.Y.: AV2 by Weigl, 2017.

Meister, Cari. *Do You Really Want to Meet an Anteater?* Mankato, Minn.: Amicus Ink, 2019.

Schuh, Mari. *Aardvark or Anteater?* Minneapolis, Minn.: Bellwether Media, 2023.

ON THE WEB

FACTSURFER

Factsurfer.com gives you a safe, fun way to find more information.

1. Go to www.factsurfer.com.

2. Enter "giant anteaters" into the search box and click 🔍.

3. Select your book cover to see a list of related content.

Index

ants, 12
cars, 8, 19
Central America, 5
climate change, 10, 20
deforestation, 14
donations, 20
ecosystems, 12
farmers, 9, 10, 16, 17
fields, 10, 16
fires, 10, 16
food, 13
forage, 6
forests, 6
governments, 14
grasslands, 6, 14
habitats, 6, 10
home ranges, 17
homes, 7, 8, 15
hunt, 9
land, 9, 17
laws, 14

people, 7, 9, 18
range, 7
roads, 8, 18
size, 5
snouts, 4, 5
South America, 5
species, 5
stats, 11
termites, 12
threats, 9
ways to help, 20
wildlife groups, 20
world with, 13

The images in this book are reproduced through the courtesy of: Andre Goncalves, front cover; Eric Isselee, p. 3; pixel creator, p. 4; Lauren Bilboe, pp. 5, 6; slowmoitiongli, p. 8; T photography, p. 9 (top left); Tarcisio Schnaider, p. 9 (top right); Azahara Perez, p. 9 (bottom); blickwinkel/ Alamy Stock Photo, p. 10; MJ Photography/ Alamy Stock Photo, pp. 10-11; Octavio Campos Salles/ Alamy Stock Photo, pp. 12. 20-21; tjakab, p. 13 (top right); Dr Morley Read, p. 13 (top right); Ben Latham, p. 13 (bottom); Ian Fox, p. 14; miroslav chytil, p. 15; Alf Ribeiro, p. 16; TashaBubo, p. 17; Panther Media GmbH/ Alamy Stock Photo, p. 18; Vladislav T. Jirousek, p. 19; Sergey Novikov, p. 20; OHishiapply, p. 22.